Grand Teton

A Guide to
Grand Teton National Park
Wyoming

Produced by the
Division of Publications
National Park Service

U.S. Department of the Interior
Washington, D.C. 1984

Part 1

Welcome to the Tetons

What Gratitude We Owe

By Margaret E. Murie

A bronze plaque at the doorway of the Maude Noble Cabin on the banks of the Snake River at Moose, Wyoming, recounts a notable meeting in 1923. It was a meeting at which "... Mr. Struthers Burt, Dr. Horace Carncross, Mr. John L. Eynon, Mr. J. R. Jones and Mr. Richard Winger, all residents of Jackson Hole, presented to Mr. Horace Albright, then Superintendent of Yellowstone National Park, a plan for setting aside a portion of Jackson Hole as a National Recreation Area for the use and enjoyment of the people of the United States."

The plaque commemorates both the beginning and the end of a stormy period—from 1918 on into the 1950s—in Jackson Hole's history. Those meeting at Miss Noble's simple log cabin wanted to devise a way to save the valley's natural beauty from commercial exploitation. They wanted it protected by a public agency. These few people recognized the need for safeguarding a meaningful segment of our country from the uses of commerce. Their idea did not catch on immediately.

In 1926 Horace Albright escorted John D. Rockefeller, Jr., and family into Jackson Hole, and a bright hope for this valley was born. Albright imparted to Rockefeller his vision of the whole valley as a national park. Rockefeller said nothing then but later admitted that Albright's vision had set his own dreams in motion. A land company was formed to shield Rockefeller's involvement, and it began to purchase valley parcels. Unaware of this, Congress voted to create a Grand Teton National Park in 1929. The park was only about one-third the size of today's park, protecting only the immediate mountain range, and very little of the valley floor.

The 150 square miles of mostly mountain land then comprising Grand Teton National Park were not enough to safeguard the complete ecosystem of the valley. Through his agents, Rockefeller quietly purchased ranches and other private lands in upper

The Teton Range's sharp rise off the valley floor provides spectacular scenery and easy access. A day hike puts you right in the mountains.

Pages 4-5: *The Grand Teton, the heart of the range, rises to 13,770 feet in elevation.*

Jackson Hole, where the soil was not good for ranching and some ranchers were having a hard time. In the avowed purpose of later turning them over to the Federal Government, Rockefeller was carrying out the aims of those who had met at Maude Noble's cabin. And through all the following stormy years; through the establishment by proclamation of Franklin D. Roosevelt of the Jackson Hole National Monument to contain the Rockefeller-purchased lands; through all the opposition to it; through the eventual negotiated "peace" and the addition of all the monument lands to Grand Teton National Park by Congress in 1950, the Rockefeller family held to its goal of "a complete project."

So now, after all the years and all the tumult, the cattlemen have their grazing rights on the national forest lands and the right to drift their cattle across national park lands to reach those permits; people still have their homes, dudes still come to the dude ranches. No one, Oldtimer or Newcomer, would now deny that the national park has vitalized the economy of the valley a thousandfold. These material results are quite obvious. Our problem now is not the amount of lands that are under State, private, or Federal jurisdiction, but whether or not we can keep our souls receptive to the message of peace these unspoiled lands offer us.

In my many years living in this valley called Jackson Hole, I have sometimes had half-waking fantasies about how such a very special place came to be. One could almost imagine that 50 or 60 million years ago some great force purposely set about to create a valley as beautiful as any valley could be. A step further into fantasy, one might imagine this great force saying: "Let us start, of course, with mountains. I shall raise up a block of granite from the Earth planet's interior; over the centuries it will become a magnificent 14,000 feet high; time and the winds and waters will sculpt it. Looking across to it will be other hills and mountains, and glaciers will form the valley and then melt away and there will be waters and streams flowing through. But with only the winds and waters singing, it will be too quiet, it will not be alive, so there must be animals—mammals, birds, fish, frogs, toads, butterflies, and all the rest."

Fritiof Fryxell, the first ranger naturalist of the park, has described the forming of these peaks:

For many birding enthusiasts the park's scenery proves merely a dividend. They come to see the stately trumpeter swan, the largest waterfowl species in North America, which nests in the park. Grand Teton and Yellowstone National Parks provide essential habitat for this bird's survival.

Pages 8-9: Broad, cupped antlers—in velvet here—and an oversized muzzle positively identify the moose.

Pages 10-11: The world of winter comes to the range and valley with indescribable grace and stillness.

"With continued uplift came a stage when the passing air currents, in surmounting the block, were compelled to rise so high that their moisture condensed. Precipitation over the elevated region was thereby increased. The streams, ever gaining in volume and velocity, now flowed along with the fine enthusiasm and vigor of youth, and like a group of skilled artisans singing at their work, went about their business of sculpturing the range."

Within this space the Creator must have intended to bring man in humility to his knees. Imagine traveling into the range from either south or north, toward its center. The peaks loom ever higher and steeper and more dramatic until, as Fryxell points out, with the 6.5 kilometers (4 miles) between Avalanche and Cascade, two of the canyons piercing the range, there stand in close ranks the South, Middle, and Grand Teton, Mt. Owen, Teewinot, Nez Perce, Cloudveil Dome, and many spires. These form an overwhelming Gothic assemblage of peaks, a concentrated and unforgettable mountain experience for anyone. And it all goes on, and on, and on, north or south, from there.

This is the Teton Range, but it is not the whole picture. The glaciers that during the Ice Age came through the whole valley left lakes as a row of jewels at the feet of the peaks: Phelps, Taggart, Bradley, Jenny, Leigh, and then finally Jackson lakes, through which the Snake River travels for some 17 miles southward. From the lakes the flat glacial floor extends to meet the river in mid-valley and beyond to all the other beautiful, though not quite so spectacular, mountains and hills that form the north, east, and south walls of the valley known as Jackson Hole.

Those "other mountains" are the Yellowstone Plateau to the north, the Absaroka, the Washakie, and Gros Ventre, merging southward into the Hoback and Snake River Ranges. It is immediately clear why the first mountain men called this type of valley a hole. As the Snake winds its way south from its source in a high mountain meadow in southern Yellowstone National Park, into and out of Jackson Lake, it is joined by other streams: Pacific Creek, the Buffalo River, the Gros Ventre. All are bordered by cottonwood and aspen and spruce and fir forests. The scene is one of infinite variety, and in summer it is aglow with wildflowers of every hue. When I first entered the valley in mid-July of 1927, I thought surely I was entering a fairyland.

We know that for many hundreds of years the Indians came to this valley to hunt and fish, but not to stay. They left the land nearly untouched. Then in the early 1800s came the mountain men to harvest the beaver. And the valley became the favorite of one David Jackson, for whom it was named by his fur trade partner, William Sublette, in 1829, 100 years before Grand Teton National Park was established.

The first white settlers came to the hole about 1884, settling first in the southern part of the valley. Grass grew there and hay could be raised. Cattle could live there. But it was a demanding environment. The settlers worked hard all summer and battled cold and deep snow in winter, feeding their stock by horse-drawn sleigh or on snowshoes. Much could be written about their survival techniques, but what interests us here in connection with the national park is that the life they led nurtured a bold and independent spirit. They believed in their "first rights" to this part of the world, and resisted anything threatening their independence and proprietary feelings. Most of what is now the national park was part of Teton National Forest in 1929, and cattlemen had grazing rights on the forest. Naturally they were flamingly opposed to anything that might change their privileges. This was the human background for the long drama of saving a good portion of Jackson Hole in its natural state, for the benefit of untold generations of people from all over the world.

Teton country was a part of the West where, thankfully, gold was not an issue. An oldtimer once left this notice on a Snake River gravel bar:

Author Mardy Murie and her late husband, Olaus, came to Jackson Hole for his now world famous elk studies. Her home base is still in Jackson Hole, although she travels across North America in the cause of conservation.

>*Payin gold will never be found here*
>*No matter how many men tries*
>*There's some enough to begile one*
>*Like tanglefoot paper does flies.*

That left cattle as the only "gold," with their owners ready to fight for what they considered their rights. The puzzling yet invigorating diversity among people is part of the long evolution of the human spirit. Jackson Hole was and still is a fascinating micro-

cosm reflecting these diversities, and they all played roles in the long controversy that colors the history of this great national park.

One of the valley's most famous residents, author Struthers Burt, once wrote: "I am afraid for my own country unless some help is given it—some wise direction. It is too beautiful and now too famous. Sometimes I dream of it unhappily."   When Burt wrote this there had irrupted at Jenny Lake and nearby, in front of the most impressive view of the main Teton peaks, a gasoline station, tourist cabins, a hot dog stand, a dance hall, and some rusting bodies of automobiles. No wonder he dreamed unhappily. But "some wise direction" did come. All the old blight along the highway has been removed and today there is a small ranger station, a tents-only campground, camper store, a small visitor center, and a small boat dock.

"The American public will not leave Jackson Hole alone; nor can we ask them to," my husband, Olaus, wrote in 1943. "They will be coming in increasing numbers. In any situation involving large numbers of us, some regulation becomes a necessity, whether we like it or not. . . . It should be our ambition to assist all agencies to keep intact this one segment of America that we boast of as 'the last of the Old West.' "

The Indians hunted and fished in this valley for all those hundreds of years and left no mark. The white man has been here less than one hundred and has left many marks. Today we have enlarged Grand Teton National Park, and the staff of the park now copes with a flow of nearly three million visitors each year.

On the edges and outskirts of the park, we still have the cloud of what Robert Righter describes in his history of the park as "the threats of subdivision and mammonism." Righter bemoans the damper such activities can put on the human spirit otherwise inspired by the mountain range. "It seems important," he says, "that future generations know that the Park commemorates not only the grandeur of nature but also the spirit of men acting for a noble cause; it is a park not of chance but of man's design."

Today, come to this national park with an open mind, open eyes, and an open heart. Leave your conveyance; walk the trails up into the canyons,

Pages 16-17: *Aspens gone golden for autumn stand reflected in the Snake River.*

Pages 18-19: *The few remaining Jackson Hole ranches reflect the Old West.*

around the lakes, into the hills, canoe on some of the lakes. Stand quietly at dusk by a beaver pond and you may see a moose or two or three, some ducks, a great blue heron, a pair of trumpeter swans. The list is long of what may be seen. And the list is equally long—or longer—of what may be heard if you stand quietly: the song of the Swainson's thrush or the ruby-crowned kinglet, the raucous conversation of ravens, the chatter of pine squirrels, the rattling call of sandhill cranes.

Go by foot or canoe or kayak or on a quiet horse or, in winter, on cross-country skis. You will sense the full and busy and yet harmonious life pattern of the wild ones. It will come to mean something very special to you, for it is a balm and a benediction. It is a reminder of your primeval roots. Stand at the edge of some woods at night and hear a great-horned owl hooting; perhaps, if you are lucky, coyotes singing; or, after September 1, some bull elk bugling.

Be glad they are all still here. These quiet adventures will remain with you always. And think then, too, what might have happened in this valley, and what gratitude we owe a few.

Part 2

Teton Country

The Mountains

The tight concentration of tall peaks and pinnacles called the Cathedral Group has been described as "Chartres multiplied by six, a choir of shimmering granite spires soaring high above the nave and transept of the valley below." Few fail to be impressed by these most scenic of mountains and by their staggering panoramic quality. Theodore Roosevelt, so often given to eloquence, called this "the most beautiful country in the world." You may find yourself spending an inordinate amount of time just staring at the mountains.

The Tetons, being classic fault-block mountains, were originally mound-like, not jagged and spired. They were formed as the Earth cracked along a north-south line at the base of the mountains. As the Earth's outer crust faulted under pressures deep within its mantle, the western block tilted upward and the eastern block sank. We speak about this mountain building in the past tense because, for us mortals, mountains symbolize eternity. But the action continues.

The Tetons are the youngest mountains in the Rocky Mountain system, but they are made out of some of the oldest rock in North America. The granitic gneisses and schists north and south of the central, highest peaks are some of the hardest and least porous rocks known. The rock of the Grand Teton is a younger granite. These qualities, and the accessibility of major peaks, attract technical rock climbers. The handholds are secure and the views breathtaking.

The geologic time scale is so vast we cannot imagine it. Most of us simply refuse to imagine more than a few thousand years; we find anything greater too inhibiting. The Ice Age ended its major glacial action about 10,000 years ago, the beginning of the Holocene or the Recent, as early man wandered the glacial ice margins. But seven-eighths of Earth history are tied up in the Precambrian Period, the period of formation of the Teton Range's 3.5-billion-year-old rocks. By contrast, just east of Jackson Hole—Thermopolis on your Wyoming highway map—there is now forming the youngest rock in the United States, travertine. Further proof that geologic processes continue.

The massive Teton Range contains a miniaturized world on a different time scale. The alpine world is a summer surprise because it offers flowering displays

Mount Moran looms as the backdrop to a forested slope in autumn.

Pages 22-23: *The Greater Yellowstone Ecosystem supports the largest elk herd remaining in the world. Nearly 3,000 of these majestic animals, also called wapiti, summer in Grand Teton.*

long after the valley show concludes for the season. Bloom time is delayed by ascending altitude: the rule of thumb is about 12 days delay per 1,000 feet. If you miss the yellow buttercups at lower elevations, climb higher and you may overtake their montane flowering in full bloom. Such are the rigors of alpine tundra life that here the flowers largely depend on wind for pollination, or on flies, rather than on bees. Bees cannot withstand the cold temperatures so common at these heights. The alpine insect explosion is brief, but ants, ladybugs and other beetles, and diminutive grasshoppers inhabit the alpine world. They make fast food for alpine-nesting birds, such as pipits, horned larks, white-crowned sparrows, and rosy finches that are desperately trying to nourish their hungry broods between the two edges of winter.

Specialized and severe, the alpine world is sparsely populated. Here eagles and weasels hunt for bird nestlings, marmots, pikas, pocket gophers, deer mice, and voles. The heartbeat of the extremely fragile tundra is slow by necessity. That any plants have adapted to this environment seems incredible. Yet alpine laurel fills rock crevices. Spring beauty blooms in pockets of soil. Mats of moss campion carpet slopes of shattered rock. White columbine nod in the wind shadows of larger rocks. Alpine sunflowers blaze like a galaxy of equal suns, their disproportionately large flowers awkwardly seated on abbreviated stalks.

The process of developing from bare rock to fully developed alpine vegetation might require thousands of years. By contrast, it is estimated that 100 years are required to form one inch of soil on the plains. On alpine heights the rate is many times slower. The first plants to colonize bare mountain rock might be lichens, multi-colored crustose plants adapted to extreme conditions. Lichens are tough. They grow on rocky outcrops near the South and North Poles. They also thrive on desert rocks that are too hot to touch. Lichen plants can first be dried in air and then in a dessicator and then exposed to 514°F for up to seven hours and yet, upon return to room temperatures, they will resume normal metabolism. And lichens regulate, to some extent, water flow at high elevations. On dry days their water content may be from two to ten percent of dry weight. On rainy days that may soar to more than 300 percent. Mats of lichen hold so much moisture that even a rise in barometric pressure may press some water out to resume its tortuous trip toward the Pacific Ocean.

Seven Teton peaks exceed 12,000 feet and one, the Grand Teton, pushes above 13,000 feet to 13,770 feet in elevation. At such heights, conditions support mountain glaciers. The Teton Glacier is one of about a dozen small alpine glaciers cradled in shaded east- or north-facing cirques among the high peaks. Teton Glacier occupies a spectacular cirque that faces east between the north face of the Grand and Mount Owen. It is partially fed by avalanches from the cliffs around it. Some of these cliffs are more than 3,000 feet high. The glacier's terminus has retreated markedly since 1929, but the rate of loss was less between 1954 and 1963 than it was between 1929 and 1954. The mountain glaciers in today's Tetons are not left over from the Ice Age. They began forming about 500 to 1,000 years ago, during the so-called Little Ice Age.

As insignificant as these glaciers are compared to the colossal sheets that repeatedly lumbered through the Tetons and Jackson Hole, they slowly exact a toll on this hard rock, continuing to carve, etch, and abrade the range. They host life too: algae of a reddish hue that give rise to the phenomenon called watermelon snow.

The Teton Range

Any mountain range is the product of the struggle between uplift and erosion, but in few places are the results as clear as on the crest of the Teton Range. Today we do not first see the Teton peaks across 160 kilometers (100 miles) of wilderness and then struggle to them afoot, on horseback, or by wagon. This spectacle may break upon us from the window of an airplane, or appear around a bend in the John D. Rockefeller, Jr. Memorial Parkway. The telescoping of time does not lessen the impact however. The range's nearly even east base (see painting) is the best place from which to grasp its formation. Along this line the valley ends at an abrupt wall, with no foothills at the mountain's base. These are sure signs of faulting, the elevation of a mountain block along a deep crack in the Earth's crust. (See top diagram, page 31.) Shatter lines visible in many of the naked rock peaks show that the uplift was no smooth ride. The Tetons are very young mountains composed of very old rock. The range was thrust up about 9 million years ago. Young? Yes, when compared to the main Rocky Mountains, which rose 60 million years ago, and the Great Smoky Mountains, which have been above water more than 200 million years. The Teton Range's crystalline rock is comparable to the 3-billion-year-old Allegheny Mountains core. This hard, stable rock, more than 300 times older than the mountains it forms, is a boon to climbers.

Grand Teton

1 · 2 · 3 · 4 · 5 · 6 · 7 · 8 · 10

Taggart Lake · Bradley Lake · Jenny Lake

JACKSON HOLE

Snake River

Another unusual feature of the Teton Range is its divide, the division line at which water will flow off the mountains either west into the Teton River or east into the Snake. The Teton's divide lies well below and to the west of the highest elevation. This is because the steeper east face caused water to flow off faster and thereby to cut deeper. These streams carved into the range and captured headwaters from less erosive western streams. Erosion and uplift continue competing in the range, which still rises through periodic earthquake activity.

1. Mount Wister
2. Shadow Peak
3. South Teton
4. Cloudveil Dome
5. Nez Perce Peak
6. Middle Teton
7. Mount Owen
8. Teewinot Mountain
9. Rockchuck Peak
10. Mount St. John
11. The Jaw
12. Mount Woodring
13. Maidenform Peak
14. Mount Moran
15. Window Peak
16. Bivouac Peak

TETON   BASIN

1

13

12

14

15

16

Leigh Lake

Jackson Lake

Forming and Shaping the Mountains

Uplift, erosion, and glaciation formed and shaped the Teton Range. Ice Age glaciers profoundly sculpted the horn-shaped peaks and gouged out the U-shaped valleys (photo and bottom diagram). The present mountain glaciers were formed only 500 to 1,000 years ago.

The Teton Range is a textbook example of fault-block mountain building (diagram at right). The Teton Fault is about 40 miles long. Total vertical displacement was about 30,000 feet. Erosion

has removed some 3,000 feet of material from Mount Moran, whose peak now stands about 6,600 feet above the valley floor. Most of the displacement took place with the dropping of the eastern block. The Range's steep east face eroded faster than the western slope, which still carries some capping sedimentary layers.

*As massive Ice Age glaciers flowed through the Teton Range (**below**), moving ice changed the steep, V-shaped,*

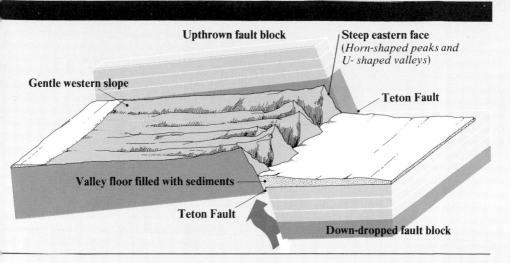

Upthrown fault block

Steep eastern face
(*Horn-shaped peaks and U- shaped valleys*)

Gentle western slope

Teton Fault

Valley floor filled with sediments

Teton Fault

Down-dropped fault block

water-cut valleys (left) into the distinctive U-shaped can-yons seen today.

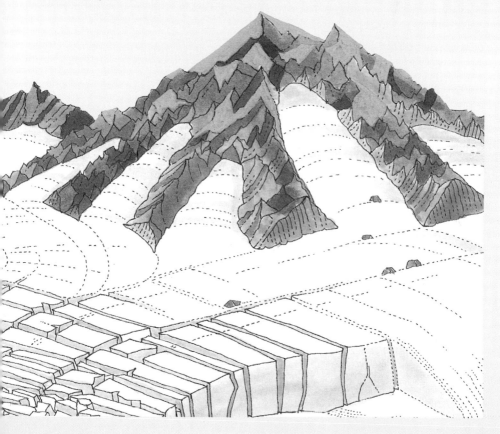

Teton Country Lakes

With only a brief itinerary in the park you might leave Jackson Hole with a memory of the high peaks and just one lake, much the impression that postcards give. But there are dozens of lakes. Most must be sought off the highway behind fringes of trees or up a short reach of trail. Some nestle in the alpine heights. A checklist of park lakes based on how they were formed includes surprising variety. A few are oxbow lakes, cut off meanders of the Snake River. Two are real oldtimers,

Emma Matilda and Two Ocean Lakes, formed about 30,000 years ago as the glaciers melted back. But most are new glistening souvenirs of the latest glacial advance that ended 8,000 years ago. This newest crop is readily identified by the morainal dams that back up each lake. Most easily recognized is the morainal dam of Jenny Lake. Unlike Jackson (large photo), Jenny, Bradley, Taggart, Leigh, and Phelps Lakes mark surfaces gouged by mountain glaciers. The many small

ponds dotting the sagebrush flats, such as The Potholes, are not gouge scars, but pits. Here glacial outwash materials surrounded and buried small ice masses that later melted. The technical term for these depression ponds is kettle ponds, but The Potholes were named by a rancher, not a geologist. The Tetons' highest lakes are called tarns (inset photo). Bearing names such as Surprise, Grizzly Bear, Bearpaw, and Rimrock, these are diminutive versions of the

glacial lakes at the foot of major canyons. They originate in ice-scoured pockets and are still forming under the small glaciers at the heads of highcountry canyons. The largest and most heavily fished lake is Jackson Lake. Cutthroat trout are native, but lake trout (Mackinaw) were introduced in the 19th century. The lake is 130 meters (425 feet) deep and 26 kilometers (16 miles) long. Jackson, a natural lake, was dammed before the park was established, to store more water

and control the Snake River for irrigation in Idaho. The Teton country's lake and pond environment has benefited moose and ducks the most, but nearly all park denizens—vacationing *Homo sapiens* included—appreciate this aquatic resource. One species, the beaver, extends its appreciation by creating more ponds. Once nearly exterminated during the trapper's era, beaver are now abundant here.

The Tetons offer the adventurous some of North America's most superb mountain climbing. The rock is very hard and mostly free of slides. Cracks and ledges abound for hand and foot holds. The mountains, rising sharply from the valley floor, are unusually accessible. No expedition is required just to reach the peak. All Teton peaks and spires have already been climbed. Many have been climbed by several routes. Together they offer an exceptional range of

climbing difficulty, from a stiff uphill walk with little hand and foot work to technical climbs that challenge most experienced alpinists. Atop the 4,200-meter (13,770-foot) summit of the Grand Teton you stand taller than anything nearby. (A climbing permit is required. See "Mountaineering" in Part 3.)

This print, adapted from Leigh Ortenburger's 1956 A Climber's Guide to the Teton Range, shows the Grand Teton from the northeast. The four climbing routes indicated, and their first-ascent dates, are: 1 East Ridge (1929), 2 Northeast Couloir (1939), 3 North Face (1936), and 4 North Ridge (1931).

First climbed (officially) in 1898, the Grand was not climbed again until 1923.

Since then, however, it has been one of the country's most popular peaks.

The first ascent by a Jackson Hole woman. Geraldine Lucas, aged 59, is shown here in her triumphant moment in 1924.

Officially, the first party to climb the Grand Teton was the W. O. Owen party in 1898, although Hayden Survey members James Stevenson and Nathaniel Langford said they climbed it in 1872. Owen carried on a 30-year war to have history rewritten his way. He finally won—by act of the Wyoming legislature in 1929.

Even a member of Owen's party thought Stevenson and Langford had climbed it. And among Owen's papers at his death was an 1899 letter, with route map, from a man who evidently climbed the Grand in 1893 with two soldiers. The man was not interested in particular credit for it.

Above the tree limit and around snowfields and glaciers lies the alpine tundra. This fragile ecosystem challenges plant and animal survival with temperature extremes, high winds, a short growing season, frequent drought, and poor soil. Basic plant survival adaptations include dwarfism, oversize root systems, matting growth, succulent leaves or stems, and warmth-producing red pigments. Some high mountain plants are almost brown, not green, but perfectly alive.

Dwarfism and matting keep plants snugged low to the ground where conditions are less severe than just a few centimeters higher. Animals tend to adapt to subalpine and alpine rigors by modifying their behavior rather than their structure. Exceptions include flightless grasshoppers and the pika's fur-covered feet.

The summer alpine tundra (**below**) provides insects, seeds, leaf crops, lichens, and fungi as wildlife food. For this short season animals are well supplied and may become conspicuous. Birds, with their advantage of flight, can cover vast areas quickly in the search for food. They can also readily change ecozones. A bird flying from alpine tundra down to a forested slope makes a journey between ecozones equivalent to migrating from above the Arctic Circle to northern Maine. Hawks and eagles, in a regular search for pikas or mice, can cover all of the Teton high peaks in 2 hours or less.

Plants and animals of the mountain world:

1 *Prairie falcon*
2 *Pika*
3 *Yellow-bellied marmot*
4 *Cushion buckwheat*
5 *Whitebark pine*
6 *Subalpine fir krummholz*
7 *Dwarf willow*
8 *Pixie-cup lichen*
9 *Black rosy finch*
10 *Alpine forget-me-not*
11 *Moss campion*
12 *Haircap moss*

Wary bighorn sheep (photo at left) are the largest mammals of the high mountain realms. The male's horns, curved back, down, and around, may cap a 135-kilogram (300-pound) body. Sheep wear thick, tannish-gray hair. Their specialized footpads enable them to scale rock that might stymie a roped alpinist. Rams and ewes hold to separate bands except during the mating period. Generations of sheep will occupy the same range. The Teton population, numbering between 100 and 125 animals, is wary because the sheep are hunted in fall on adjacent national forest lands. Hikers and climbers occasionally see them on the range's east side, but you will not see bighorn sheep from your car except sometimes in the winter when they may move down into Jackson Hole.

The Valley

With the Louisiana Purchase treaty signed, President Thomas Jefferson wanted to know what he had bought, so he sent the Lewis and Clark Expedition overland to the Pacific in 1803 to find out. On the return trip John Colter left the expedition along the Yellowstone River to stay in the West and join a trapping venture. He is considered the first white person to discover what is now Jackson Hole. Colter supposedly wandered through this high, mountain-encircled valley — trappers called such valleys holes — in the winter of 1807-1808. Colter was soon followed by other trappers, and 40 years later the trappers were followed by homesteaders. Several homesteaders became dude ranchers, and their dudes were followed by vacationers, who now number nearly three million each year.

The flatness of Jackson Hole comes as a surprise, considering that the Teton Range was formed by a fault-block process. You would expect a deep valley, but it has been filled repeatedly by rock debris transported by glaciers and their meltwaters. The Snake River does little cutting into the valley floor today. The flat areas above the river, called benches, were carved out when the river had the torrential force of glacial meltwater. The river's north-south flow shows that the valley slopes southward. The valley also tilts westward, toward the fault that gave rise to the Teton Range. For reasons not fully known, the valley has sunk more than the mountains have risen. We know this because a sedimentary cap of rock atop Mount Moran — nearly 6,000 feet above the valley floor — was once connected to the same rock layer that now lies an estimated 24,000 feet below the valley surface.

The glacial material that fills the valley is largely quartzite rock rounded by tumbling in running water into softball- to basketball-sized cobbles, supplemented by gravel, sand, and silt. This rock came from long-vanished mountains to the northwest. The depth of the valley's cobble material is estimated at perhaps about 2,000 feet. This cobble material has been washed by glacial runoff so often that it lacks the clay content that is essential for the ground to retain water. Melting snow and rain rapidly percolate through, so that only grasses and other plants adapted to arid conditions can thrive in the valley's coarse-textured soil. This is why sagebrush domi-

Autumn aspens lend what prospectors never found in this valley — large touches of gold.

Pages 40-41: *The Snake River meanders through the surprisingly flat valley called Jackson Hole.*

Jackson Hole was settled around the turn of the century, initially by homesteaders.

John D. Rockefeller, Jr., donated more than 32,000 acres of valley land, which were added to Grand Teton National Park in 1950.

Local residents were divided over the park issue. Two local park proponents, Mardy and the late Olaus J. Murie, are shown at a 1949 annual council meeting of the Wilderness Society. The Muries advocated park enlargement.

nates the valley floor, except where streams and ponds provide enough water for willow bushes, spruce, and cottonwood trees. Lodgepole pines grow atop the recent glacial moraines that contain sufficient nutrients and clay, such as the one surrounding Jenny Lake.

Geologic forces have not always been subtle influences in the valley. Melting snow and heavy rains in June 1925 saturated a layer of clay sandwiched between sedimentary rock layers that form the north end of Sheep Mountain, near Kelly. An earthquake, probably, triggered an enormous landslide, and thousands of tons of debris raced down into the river, damming it and backing up a lake 5 miles long and 200 feet deep. Two years later the top 50 feet of the dam broke off and a wall of water rushed down through Kelly, leveling all buildings except the church and school. Six lives were lost, despite ample warning. The landslide scar on Sheep Mountain's north end is more than 5,000 feet long and 2,500 feet wide. Geologists say that more of Sheep Mountain is perched to slide, given similar spring rainfall and an earthquake trigger.

The rise of the Teton Range and the corresponding sinking of Jackson Hole continues, although not at an even rate. The action continues by irregular crustal movements known as earthquakes. Geologist John D. Love, longtime interpreter of the dynamics of the Teton Range, feels that a major earthquake movement along the Teton fault, of as much as 20 feet, could happen at any time. The impact would be many more times severe than the landslide and ensuing flood at Kelly. But such things are not given to easy and precise prediction.

The Jackson Hole elk herd is free ranging and migratory. About half of its 15,000 elk winter on the National Elk Refuge. By midsummer, many graze on bunchgrass in high meadows near the Continental Divide, more than 110 kilometers (70 miles) to the north. Moving north in spring, the elk feed on succulent new growth of grasses and forbs in the sagebrush flats. Cow elk, pregnant since last fall, separate from the main herds to linger on calving grounds. Newborn elk hide in sage-brush or aspen cover while the cows feed. Elk tend to feed in the open in morning and evening, retreating to forest shade during the day. All summer they gain weight in preparation for winter. Full grown cows often exceed 230 kilograms (500 pounds). Bulls may stand 1.5 meters (5 feet) at the shoulder and weigh 405 kilograms (900 pounds). After their antlers drop off in March, bulls begin growing a new annual set. Antlers, furry nubbins in May, become velvet covered branches by July.

By late August the velvet, which supplied blood and nutrients for rapid antler growth, hangs in tattered shreds as bull elk rub their antlers against flexible saplings. In September, mature bulls polish the velvet from their antlers and join the cows on their summer ranges. Then the dominant bull elk gather harems of 6 to 20 cows. These bulls establish and maintain dominance by displaying massive branched antlers, impressive bugling, chasing off less aggressive bulls, and occasional combat with other males. Fall migratory herds sometimes number 200 or more. Migration begins when the snow reaches a critical depth. It is a special experience to witness this exodus of elk streaming down the valley. Many elk return to winter on the National Elk Refuge and in the Gros Ventre drainage. Supplemental feeding is provided on the refuge to maintain the Jackson Hole herd because some two-thirds of its traditional winter range has been lost to development. The remaining habitat, and the elk hunt permitted by the law that added Jackson Hole to the national park, is cooperatively managed by the National Park Service and other Federal and State agencies to perpetuate and protect the majestic elk of this great herd.

45

Settling the Valley

Shoshone, Crow, Blackfeet, Gros Ventre, and other Native Americans hunted and picked berries in the valley in summer, but winter was unbearable. During the early 1800s, solitary mountain men trapped valley beaver, sometimes wintering through intense and deep snow. After the fur trade collapsed in 1840, occasional trappers and prospectors ventured into Jackson Hole. Well-known pioneers built temporary cabins. Jackson Hole was settled late in the frontier era, when limited technology, supply routes, and food storage made winter bearable. The first permanent settlers, John Holland and John Carnes, homesteaded north of the town of Jackson in 1884. Significant settlement came after 1900 as schools, post offices, and churches were built. Jackson, Wilson, Moran, and Kelly became the dominant communities. Getting supplies and mail into Jackson Hole was always difficult. Most supplies came from Idaho over rugged Teton

Pass. Pack horses and supply wagons then faced the Snake River, often dangerous or impossible to cross. Menor's Ferry, built at Moose in 1894 by William D. Menor, was a major crossing until replaced by a bridge in 1927. Ferries, and later bridges, at Wilson also improved valley transportation. Most valley homesteaders became cattle ranchers, grazing their herds on the public range and cultivating enough hay for winter feed. But the harsh climate and porous soils made ranching risky. When some ranchers recognized the value of scenery and wildlife, they began operating dude ranches and hunting lodges. In 1903, Ben Sheffield catered to wealthy hunters from his headquarters at Moran. In 1907, Louis Joy operated the first dude ranch in Jackson Hole, the JY. The age of tourism had begun. The large photo shows a rodeo at the Elbo Ranch, which was located near Cottonwood Creek.

The Snake River

Grand Teton National Park and Jackson Hole have no corner on the Snake River, boasting as they do a mere 40 miles or so of the sinuous Snake's more than 1,000 miles of progress from the Continuental Divide near Yellowstone National Park to its confluence with the mighty Columbia River near Pasco, Washington.

Judging from its almost leisurely mid-summer passage as a braided river through the park you would not guess what chaos lies downstream. The river had at least two names before the Snake was affixed. A group of French-speaking trappers who crossed the river in September 1811 encountered such difficulty they decided to give it the name Mad River. Sometime later this trapping party had to cross it again downstream near its confluence with the Hoback River and renamed it *La Maudite Rivière Enragée* — Accursed Mad River. Those names properly hint at what lies downstream as the Snake flows in every direction but east in a great sickle-shaped curve, its watershed embracing the largest chunk of wilderness in the United States outside Alaska. The Snake's beautiful Shoshone Falls in Idaho is a full 43 feet higher than Niagara Falls. And the Snake's Hells Canyon, also in Idaho, is North America's deepest and narrowest major gorge, averaging a deeper gash across the land than the Grand Canyon itself. Hells Canyon plunges 7,900 feet at its deepest point. What is more, it averages 5,500 feet deep over its course.

In a valley this high (the elevation of Jackson Hole at the lower end measures 6,000 feet) the Snake should have cut, with its steep gradients, permanent channels. Instead, it still wanders in myriad channels across the glacial debris filling the fault basin. Here the Snake looks more like a prairie river rambling with the restlessness of youth. Its banks are a checkerboard of successional stages, as plant communities rise and fall with disturbances created by flooding, channel shifting, or fire. This benefits the moose and beaver by assuring continual supplies of willow and cottonwood that would otherwise soon be succeeded by blue spruce.

The Snake, discovered by Lewis and Clark in 1805 but not fully explored until its headwaters were pinpointed in 1970, is no longer a completely wild river even in the park. Jackson Lake Dam, built before the park was established, controls the water

The Snake River cuts through moraines and exposes a vast rubble of glacial cobbles. An evening float trip offers an opportunity to view wildlife, a part of the river's biotic richness.

flow below the lake, moderating natural surges that used to follow rapid spring snowmelt or violent summer thunderstorms. Since the river no longer scours the valley regularly, these stabilized conditions favor the development of larger tracts of blue spruce.

Compared to the lakes, the Snake harbors a wealth of aquatic life. A river is richer partly because its linear structure provides more shoreline. The plant complex that the river makes possible continually enriches the water with leaves and other debris. This energy subsidy, along with the countless terrestrial insects caught by the river, is passed up the food chain. Eventually the additional energy is translated into the fish that help support the herons, mergansers, eagles, ospreys, otters, and other terrestrial predators that use the aquatic food pyramid.

The plant and animal composition of the riverine world varies with the rate of water flow. In slow water areas, such as the Oxbow Bend, where the river has cut off and abandoned a former looping meander, bottom-rooted aquatic plants attract herbivorous animals—moose, mallards, golden-eyes, and cinnamon teals—to graze these underwater gardens. Such quiet stretches also attract carnivores to exploit the greater variety of prey. Great blue herons stand motionless along the shoreline, waiting to spear passing fish or the mice, frogs, and snakes at water's edge. Mink and coyote patrol the shoreline.

Insects are important river denizens, as the fly fishing angler's art attests. The nymphs of mayflies and stoneflies and the larvae of caddisflies eat algae and other plant detritus, in the process becoming attractive fare for the cutthroat trout and Rocky Mountain whitefish. The caddisfly larvae have adapted to fast water by constructing protective body cases from sand grains, pebbles, plant stems, and other stream bed materials. The faster the current, the heavier the case, which enables the larvae to settle rapidly into a new cranny, should they be swept away.

The sturgeon used to populate the Snake in what are now park waters, but the erection of more than 20 hydroelectric and irrigation dams downstream so changed the river that these very large fish are now hard pressed to survive above the Columbia River confluence.

Shaped like a short-handled dipper, the Snake River progresses westward through the nation's largest chunk of wilderness outside Alaska. The Snake's drainage also figured in historic exploring expeditions and scientific, military, and railroad route surveys during the 19th century. Some important expedition and survey routes are shown on this map.

Expeditions and Trappers

Jackson Hole witnessed the exploration, settlement, and exploitation that characterized the opening of the West. Early events centered around the fur trade and survey expeditions. John Colter generally gets credit as the first white man to visit the valley, purportedly crossing it in the 1807-1808 winter. Colter trekked west with Lewis and Clark and got permission to leave them on their return east. Other trappers whose names pop up before Jackson Hole's fur trade died out in

the 1840s are Jedediah Smith, David Jackson, William Sublette, Kit Carson, and Jim Bridger. All were inveterate explorers and adventurers. Sublette probably named the valley, after his trading partner, Jackson. The fur trade died out when beaver hats—the prime pelt market—went out of fashion in Europe. By then, beaver had been severely reduced over much of North America, anyway, and a process for making felt from far cheaper rabbit pelts had been developed. The first sur-

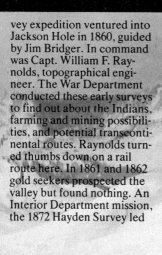

vey expedition ventured into Jackson Hole in 1860, guided by Jim Bridger. In command was Capt. William F. Raynolds, topographical engineer. The War Department conducted these early surveys to find out about the Indians, farming and mining possibilities, and potential transcontinental routes. Raynolds turned thumbs down on a rail route here. In 1861 and 1862 gold seekers prospected the valley but found nothing. An Interior Department mission, the 1872 Hayden Survey led by Professor Ferdinand V. Hayden, explored the Tetons and Jackson Hole, guided by Beaver Dick Leigh. Many Jackson Hole features are named for Hayden Survey members. These include Jenny, Bradley, Taggart, and Leigh Lakes. An expedition led by Lt. Gustavus Doane nearly perished here in the 1876-77 winter and would have starved but for the fishing skills of one private. The color illustrations are by Jackson Hole artist John Clymer: "Beaver Flats" (left) and "John Colter Visits the Crows 1807."

The Indians

No Indians made permanent, year-round homes in Jackson Hole. Winters were too severe. Before white settlement, a small, recluse Shoshone group camped in the area for as many months as possible because of repeated raids from northerly tribes who had British-supplied guns. Other Shoshone knew this small band as Sheep Eaters, because they depended on the bighorn sheep for food. They lived scattered in family groups, not as a tribe. When it seemed safe, they would fish, hunt, and gather plants, seeds, and berries. They used dogs as beasts of burden.

They made bows of elk antlers and sheep horns reinforced with elk and deer sinews. Early trappers seldom encountered the Sheep Eaters although they sometimes saw smoke from their fires. The Sheep Eaters stayed near the mountains until joining other Shoshone under Chief Washakie on reservations in Idaho and Wyoming about 1879. Some artifacts and

other evidence of their life are still found today in the Tetons. Archeological studies show that various Indian groups migrated through here on a seasonal basis. The Shoshone peoples arose in the semidesert Basin of the upper Southwest. As food became scarce they migrated east of the Rockies, into the plains and mountain parks of Wyoming and Montana, probably in the 1500s or mid-1600s. In part they were escaping slave-trading Ute Indians. By 1730, however, records begin to show the Shoshone as the most important plains tribe. They were walkers until about 1740, when they got Spanish horses from the Comanches to the south. Mounted, they would raid as far as the Saskatchewan River to the north and the Black Hills to the east. During the whites' overland migrations, the Eastern Shoshone, under Chief Washakie, avoided confrontations. But Chief Washakie knew his people's nomadic way of life was over. The inset photos show Codsiogo, a Shoshone warrior (far left), and a Sheepeater Indian family.

Cutthroat Trout

The 17 species of fish in Grand Teton National Park include brown, brook, rainbow, and lake (Mackinaw) trout. These introduced species are found in a number of lakes and streams. Perhaps the most impressive fish is the Snake River cutthroat trout, the native trout so dependent on the park's natural aquatic system. The deep red or orange-red marks under its jaws give the impression of a slashed throat, hence cutthroat. The Snake River cutthroat is a distinct subspecies

of the cutthroat trout identified by the hundreds of tiny dark spots on both sides of its body. In spring, particularly May and June, the Snake River cutthroat will travel upstream into tributary waters to spawn. The female digs a nest (called a redd) in the gravel and the male and female lie side by side while simultaneously contributing the sperm and eggs. The fertilized eggs settle to the bottom and hatch into fry within 40 days. The young fish usually remain in the tributary stream

until fall but will sometimes wait a full year before migrating to the river. Juveniles, called fingerlings, and sub-adults feed on a variety of aquatic invertebrate larvae such as caddisflies, mayflies, and stoneflies. The older fish become more predaceous and feed on a variety of smaller species of fish living in the river. The cutthroat trout reach sexual maturity at three to four years of age. Few cutthroats live longer than five years. The post-spawning mortality rate is 50 percent. The Snake River cutthroat trout indeed delights the angler, but more important is its role in the wildlife community. The cutthroat consumes aquatic insects, invertebrates, and small fish, helping to keep these populations in check naturally. This trout is also consumed, providing food for bears, eagles, ospreys, and otters. If the fish population declines, so will the animals that depend on it for food. As fishing pressure continues to grow, park managers may have to protect this natural population of Snake River cutthroat to maintain the national park's wildlife community. The inset photo shows an osprey landing on its nest.

Wildlife and Wildflowers

When the Shoshone Indians sat down with government officials at Fort Bridger in 1863 to conclude a treaty that would define their lands, the parcel that the parties arrived at totaled 30,000 square miles. A very small part of that was Jackson Hole, but this was such rich hunting ground in summer and fall that even the Shoshone dared not lay sole claim to it. Blackfeet, Bannock, Crow, Gros Ventre, and probably other tribes were drawn here to hunt. What would you have seen on a hunting trip in those days? Bison, pronghorns, and at least three times as many elk as exist here now, but far fewer deer. Near wall-to-wall beaver along the waterways, but nary a moose. And bighorn sheep peering down at you from nearly every crag and butte.

When settlement in the late 1800s at the south end of the valley eliminated about two-thirds of their winter range, as many as 500 elk sometimes ended up on the streets of Jackson on frigid nights. Winter starvation and poaching pressures took many elk.

The fur trade decimated beaver populations. But what of moose, deer, and bighorn? Moose and mule deer probably benefited from white settlement. Moose increased because of the suppression of fire, which permitted the increase of sub-alpine fir, a winter food source. Moose graze but little grass, mostly browsing coarser plants. Likewise mule deer. Livestock overgrazing hindered elk but favored moose and mule deer. The latter evidently usurped bighorn wintering range, reducing the sheep population. Wolves were extirpated and grizzly bears nearly so. That favored—within range support limits—every four-footed vegetarian not beset with other insurmountable problems.

Grizzly bears roam only the northern part of the park. Predation on large mammals must be carried out by seldom seen black bears, rare mountain lions, and coyotes, who largely feed on rodents. Red foxes (rare here), lynxes, and bobcats are crafty and formidable, but at best threaten only the young of large mammals. Formidable predators of a smaller scale are the many members of the weasel family, including two weasels, the badger, pine marten, wolverine and fisher (very rare here), and mink. The prey of these creatures includes many of the more familiar small mammals, such as shrews, hares, chipmunks and golden-mantled

Mule deer, named for their large ears, occur in surprisingly small numbers in the park. Competition with the large elk herd and deep winter snows may be limiting factors.

Pages 60-61: *The vigorous, brief blooms of alpine plants edge a high mountain meadow, with only the tips of peaks as a backdrop.*

ground squirrels, Uinta ground squirrels, red and flying squirrels, mice, pocket gophers, woodrats, voles, and muskrats, and also small birds, bird eggs, reptiles, and amphibians. Porcupines and beavers are both large rodents and both feed on bark, but their defenses differ. Beavers escape to their snug lodge protected by the surrounding water, while porcupines are protected by quills. But porcupines sometimes fall prey to fishers and maybe smaller cats and other critters able to get at their unprotected faces and bellies.

Bird watchers are content here just to see the rare trumpeter swan—on the Elk Refuge, or at Christian and Hedrick Ponds. Other large birds include bald eagles, ospreys, sandhill cranes, Canada geese, and great blue herons. The water ouzel (dipper) walks underwater in fast current, a marvel to behold. Bold and brassy are the crafty magpies, who won't hesitate to let you know if you annoy them. More than 100 species of birds have been identified in the park.

Four major natural communities provide a way of understanding the park's wildlife patterns. The water communities include lakes, ponds, rivers, and streams. The sage and grassland community is the most extensive and most often overlooked. The forest community appears randomly distributed, but soil moisture properties, the direction it faces, elevation, and weather patterns influence where trees grow. Blue spruce and cottonwood thrive along valley streams. Aspen, Douglas-fir, and lodgepole pine inhabit the valley and lower slopes. Sub-alpine fir, Englemann spruce, and limber pine stand on mountainsides and in canyons. The edges where communities meet are richest in wildlife. The alpine community crowning the highcountry shares the least characteristics and organisms with the other three communities.

Water communities call to mind perhaps the trout and beaver (see pages 48 and following), and lakes, ponds, streams, and rivers interrupt or dot the other three communities. In winter moose inhabit the river flats to browse the cottonwoods and willows.

The pronghorn and sage grouse characterize the wide open sage and grassland community, whose purpose otherwise seems simply to provide the Teton Range a foreground. This world is alive with small birds feeding on masses of insects and spiders. These songbirds, along with gophers, mice, and snakes, provide the diet for weasels, hawks, and ravens. The sage grouse depends largely on the evergreen sagebrush for food. The pronghorns depend on it part-time, being unable to subsist on grasses alone. This is North America's fastest mammal, able to run at more than 45 miles per hour. For added security it boasts oversize lungs and windpipe, and the largest eyes by body weight of any mammal. Faster yet is the prairie falcon that hunts these flats, streaking out of the sky at speeds up to 200 miles per hour.

An aspen grove of only 27 trunks may shelter more than 12 pairs of birds—house wrens, mountain bluebirds, swallows, and woodpeckers. It may also shelter an understory of young spruce and fir that could one day replace it. Deer and elk wander out of the forest to browse the aspen, which can produce more than 2.5 tons dry weight of vegetation per acre. Ironically, aspen have suffered somewhat in the park for lack of forest fires. It turns out that fire suppression suppresses aspens, which recover burned areas quickly. In respect of natural processes, the park now practices wildfire management instead of complete suppression, except where human life and private property might be threatened.

The alpine world (see pages 36-37) stands as magic for some. Its lilliputian scale fascinates. A tiny rabbit, the pika (or cony), gathers grasses there all summer in miniature haystacks you may discover. The yellow-bellied marmot, on the other hand, stores fat, its body being adapted to pass the winter in hibernation. Surprising numbers of insects are found there. And spiders wander the snowfields to feed on cold-sluggish insects blown up from warmer elevations.

Diminutive alpine creatures aren't seen from a car, but much of the park's wildlife bounty reveals itself to casual observers. The national park tries to offer the wild community a haven where natural processes can work, but this is no simple task. The park includes only portions of some creatures' annual ranges. And underlying the ideal balance of natural processes are complex relationships we only gradually unravel.

Mammals

Bobcat

Moose

Weasel

Deer mouse

Yellow-bellied marmots

Coyote

Pika

Elk calf

Badger

Mule Deer

Black bear

Uinta ground squirrel

Snowshoe hare

Beaver

Pronghorn (antelope)

Porcupine

Birdlife

Yellowthroat

Prairie falcon

Killdeer

Great gray owl

Screech owl

Sandhill crane

Blue grouse

Sage grouse

Bald eagle

Goshawk

Mountain bluebird

Canada goose

Greentail towhee

Western tanager

Steller's jay

Common snipe

Wildflowers

Columbine

Geranium

Sugarbowl

Yellow violet

Leopard lily

Phlox

Mountain or False dandelion

Low larkspur

Calypso orchid

Lewis flax

Green gentian

Harebell

Indian paintbrush

Mule ears

Yarrow

Scarlet gilia

Part 3

Guide and Adviser

Approaching Grand Teton

Grand Teton National Park sits in northwest Wyoming just below Yellowstone National Park. By road Grand Teton is reached from the north via Yellowstone on Routes 89, 191, and 287. From the east, Routes 26 and 287 connect the park with Dubois, Wyoming, via Togwotee Pass. From the south the park is reached through Jackson, Wyoming, via Routes 26, 89, and 191. Routes 191 and 189 link Jackson with Interstate 80 to the south. From the west, Route 22 over Teton Pass links Jackson with Idaho Falls, Idaho, and Interstate 15 west of Idaho Falls.

From valley floor to lofty peaks, artists face a dilemma: what not *to paint.*

Pages 70-71: *Anglers on the Snake face a similar dilemma. With each backcast, tantalizing pools and riffles vie for attention.*

Buses. The Jackson-Rock Springs Stage, (307) 733-3133, provides daily summer connections to Greyhound Bus Lines in Rock Springs, Wyoming. The address is 72 S. Glenwood, Jackson, WY 83001. From early June through mid-September the Grand Teton Lodge Company runs regular bus service between Jackson Lake Lodge and Jackson twice daily. The company also meets all incoming flights at the airport (see map) and runs a service to Signal Mountain Lodge, Colter Bay, and Jackson Lake Lodge. The company runs shuttlebuses daily between Jackson Lake Lodge and Colter Bay. Holiday Tours and Gray Line of Jackson Hole offer one-day tours of Yellowstone National Park from Jackson. Individuals may book overnight or longer passage to Old Faithful on Grayline of Jackson Hole tours, but no in-park transportation is available in Yellowstone.

Some useful distances: Denver to Grand Teton, 500 miles; Salt Lake City to Grand Teton, 288 miles: and Idaho Falls to Grand Teton, 105 miles.

Please note that public transportation to and around the park is not always regularly scheduled or frequently available. If you intend to rely on bus service for travel inside the park, plan carefully and be prepared for long waits between bus arrivals and departures in parts of the park. Hitchhiking is illegal in Wyoming.

Taxi and Transportation Services. Local taxi service is limited, but it is available. The Jackson Hole Transportation Company, (307) 733-3135, provides ground transportation for Teton Village and Jackson to and from the airport, and service to and from Flagg Ranch on the Rockefeller Parkway.

Air Service. Scheduled airlines serve the Jackson Hole Airport, 7 miles north of Jackson on Highway 26, 89, and 191. Denver, Colorado; Salt Lake City, Utah; and Idaho Falls, Idaho, all offer connecting flights to Jackson. Flights arrive and depart several times daily in summer; less frequently in the off season. Check with your travel agent for flight schedules as well as ski package rates for winter travel to the Jackson Hole area.

Car Rental Services. Avis (307) 733-3422, Budget (307) 733-2206, Hertz (307) 733-2272, and National (307) 733-4132 offer car rentals. All but Budget, which provides airport pick-up and delivery, are located at the Jackson airport.

All major park roads are two-lane and paved. Summer months coincide with road repairs and re-surfacing. It is possible to have short delays (up to one hour) while maintenance crews repair old and build new road surfaces.

Many bicyclists ride along the narrow Teton Park Road between Moose and Colter Bay (see map). Traffic is very heavy from mid-June to Labor Day and both cyclists and motorists should be alert to possible hazards.

Useful Addresses and Telephone Numbers
Grand Teton National Park, P.O. Drawer 170, Moose, WY 83012, (307) 733-2880.
Wyoming Travel Commission, Cheyenne, WY 82002, (307) 777-7777.
Jackson Hole Area Chamber of Commerce, Box E, Jackson, WY 83001, (307) 733-3316.
Grand Teton Natural History Association, P.O. Drawer 170, Moose, WY 83012, (307) 733-2880.

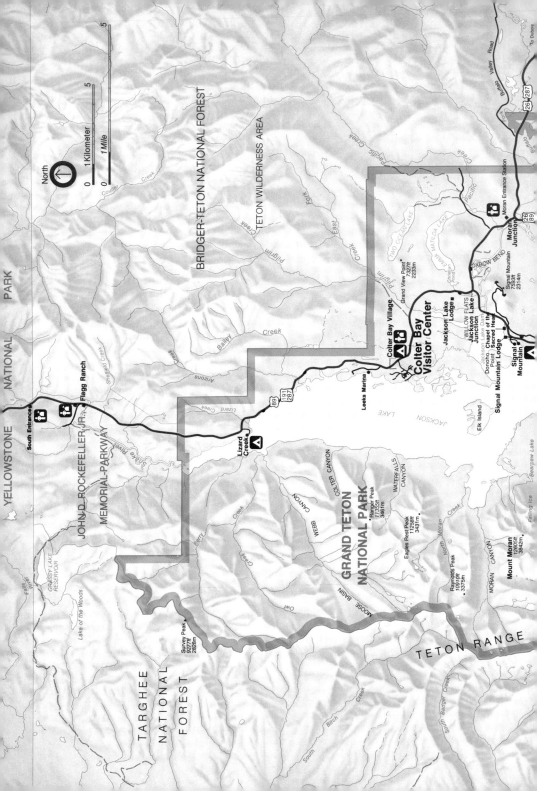

BRIDGER-TETON
NATIONAL FOREST

GROS VENTRE RANGE

Crystal Creek ▲
Crystal Creek

Red Hills ▲

Atherton Creek ▲

Gros Ventre
Slide

Grand Teton
Environmental
Education Center

Kelly

NATIONAL

ELK REFUGE

Curtis Canyon ▲

Gros Ventre ▲
Gros Ventre

Blacktail Butte
7688ft
2343m

Gros Ventre Junction

Menor's Ferry, and
Maud Noble Cabin

Moose Junction

Chapel of the
Transfiguration

MOOSE

Jackson National
Fish Hatchery

Refuge Visitor Center
Winter sleigh rides

JACKSON

Refuge Headquarters

Jackson
Information
Center

Cunningham Cabin
Historic Site

Triangle X Ranch

SHADOW MOUNTAIN

Snake River

Ditch Creek

Hedrick Pond

THE POTHOLES

North Jenny Lake
Junction
Jenny Lake Lodge

Jenny Lake
Mountaineering registration ▲

One way

Jenny Lake

Road
closed
by snow

Cottonwood Creek

TIMBERED ISLAND RIDGE

Climbers
Ranch

Moose
Entrance Station

Moose Visitor Center
Park Headquarters

Jackson
Hole
Airport

TETON NATIONAL FOREST

191

26
89

191

To I-15 and I-80

EAST GROS VENTRE BUTTE

WEST GROS VENTRE BUTTE

Snake River

Moose-Wilson Road

Moose-Wilson Road closed
to trucks, trailers, and RVs.
Road closed by snow

Teton
Village

22

Wilson

Teton Pass
8431ft
2570m

Rendezvous Peak
10927ft
3331m

Mount Hunt
10783ft
3287m

GRANITE CANYON

OPEN CANYON

Marion Lake

Moose Basin

RImrock Lake

Phelps Lake

DEATH CANYON

Buck Mountain
11938ft
3638m

AVALANCHE CANYON

Taggart Lake

Bradley Lake

GARNET CANYON

Nez Pce or Peak
11901ft
3627m

Cloudveil Dome
12026ft
3665m

Spalding
Peak

South Teton
12514ft
3814m

Middle Teton
12804ft
3903m

Grand Teton
13770ft
4197m

Mount Owen
12928ft
3940m

Teewinot Mountain
12325ft
3757m

Symmetry
Spire

CASCADE CANYON

HANGING CANYON

Cascade Creek

Mount St. John
11430ft
3484m

Hidden Falls

Teton Glacier

JENNY LAKE

String Lake

11144ft
3397m

HOLE

JACKSON

Solitude

Holly Lake

Schoolroom
Glacier

Paintbrush Canyon

ALASKA BASIN

Teton Canyon

TETON CANYON

▲ Teton

TARGHEE

NATIONAL

FOREST

Visitor Centers and Museums

To best use your time, make your first stop the Moose Visitor Center (south end) or the Colter Bay Visitor Center (north end). Ask the ranger at the desk about park activities and services. And ask for tips about what you can see and do in the time you have. You may even decide to lengthen your stay in the Tetons.

Moose Visitor Center includes information services, a publications sales outlet, and a backcountry and boating permits office. This building also houses the park headquarters and all administrative offices. Summer hours are 8 a.m. to 7 p.m.; from Labor Day to mid-May 8 a.m. to 4:30 p.m. The visitor center is on the Teton Park Road just west of Moose Junction. Check the map in advance. With such impressive scenery you can easily miss this junction.

Colter Bay Visitor Center includes the Indian Arts Museum, free film showings, a publications sales outlet, and a backcountry and boating permits office for the park's north end. Summer hours are 8 a.m. to 7 p.m.; from Labor Day to the end of September, 8 a.m. to 5 p.m.; closed from October to mid-May. Check the map in advance and watch for the sign that will direct you to the Colter Bay area and its Colter Bay Visitor Center, 6 miles north of Jackson Lake Junction and 17 miles south of Yellowstone National Park. The Indian Arts Museum there houses the extensive David T. Vernon Collection of Native American Arts. Be sure to inquire about museum tours and Indian arts and crafts activities.

At either visitor center pick up a copy of the free park newspaper, *Teewinot.* Turn to the calendar-style activities schedule and look it over at

*Colter Bay Visitor Center (**top**) serves park visitors in summer. Moose Visitor Center is open all year.*

Page 77: *The Indian Arts Museum at Colter Bay houses a large Plains Indian collection. Ranger-guided activities throughout the park provide information about its natural and human history. The Grand Teton Natural History Association sells maps and other publications to enhance your understanding of the park.*

the desk so you can get the ranger's advice on the best activities for you and your party. *Teewinot* also lists concession-operated accommodations, services, and facilities. These offer many valuable ways to experience the park. The *Teewinot* is also available at park entrance stations, campgrounds, and concession facilities.

Wayside Exhibits. As you drive through the park on the main roads, take your time and stop at the wayside turnouts along the roads. At many turnouts wayside exhibits identify the scene before you and briefly interpret the natural and human history of Jackson Hole and the Teton Range. These turnouts are usually located at excellent scenic viewpoints and provide safe parking areas for viewing and photographing the mountain scene.

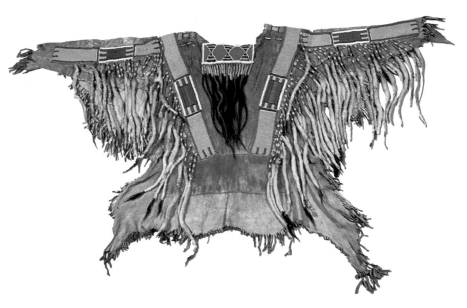

Ranger-led Activities

From mid-June through Labor Day, park rangers lead activities several times daily throughout the park. These offer ideal ways to see and understand the many natural, historical, cultural, and recreational resources the park offers. These activities are listed in *Teewinot*, the park newspaper, and are posted at each visitor center and campground. The *Teewinot* listing describes the event and tells you where and when to meet. There are short hikes, short hikes with boat transportation, all-day hikes, wildlife hikes, demonstrations, and campfire programs. Rangers present interpretive programs each night on a variety of subjects throughout the summer at the Gros Ventre, Signal Mountains, and Colter Bay Amphitheaters. All ranger-led activities are free except those requiring modest fees for supplies or transportation.

Self-guiding Trails. Informative booklets are available at visitor centers or the trailheads to guide you on short-to-modest hikes along established trails that explore the history or nature of the Tetons and Jackson Hole. These walks are great for families and provide exercise for building up to longer hikes. Self-guiding trails include: Menor's Ferry Historic Trail, Cascade Canyon Trail, Cunningham Cabin Trail, Taggart Lake Trail, Lunch Tree Hill Trail, and Colter Bay Trail.

Ranger-led hikes provide good introductions to the park. History comes alive on Menor's Ferry (middle) on the Snake River at Moose, and campers consult a field guide to identify a duck.

Camping and Accommodations

The National Park Service operates five campgrounds in the park on a first-come, first-served basis. Reservations are not accepted. A nightly fee is charged. South to north (see map) the campgrounds are: Gros Ventre, Jenny Lake, Signal Mountain, Colter Bay, and Lizard Creek. All except Jenny Lake (tents only) accommodate tents, trailers, and recreational vehicles. There are no utility hookups. All campgrounds have modern comfort stations. Maximum stay is 7 days at Jenny Lake, 14 days elsewhere. In July and August the campgrounds fill to capacity daily. Jenny Lake fills by 8 a.m.; Signal Mountain and Colter Bay fill between 10 a.m. and 1 p.m.; Lizard Creek fills between 4 and 6 p.m.; and Gros Ventre by early evening. There are trailer dumping stations at Gros Ventre, Signal Mountain, and Colter Bay. Colter Bay has showers, laundry, and propane service.

Additional camping areas are found in nearby national forests and elsewhere outside the park. Camping is not permitted along roadsides or in overlooks or parking areas. Doubling-up in campsites is prohibited. There are no overflow facilities in the park. (Backcountry campers, please see Backcountry Basics.)

Group Camping. There are 10 group camping sites at Colter Bay and five at Gros Ventre. Sites accommodate between 12 and 40 people. The nightly use fee is $1.00 per person. These are available to youth, religious, educational, and other organized groups. Reservations are required. Make them as soon as possible after January 1, by writing the chief ranger at the park address.

Trailer Villages. Concessioners operate trailer villages with full hookups, showers, and laundry at Colter Bay and Flagg Ranch (in the Rockefeller Parkway). Reservations are advised. For Colter Bay write the Grand Teton Lodge Company address (listed under Accommodations). Write to Flagg Ranch at Moran, WY 83013.

Accommodations. The many concessioners within the park offer cabins, lodge facilities, and rooms. Accommodations concessions in the park and the advance reservations telephone number (area code 307) and address are: Colter Bay Cabins, Jackson Lake Lodge, and Jenny Lake Lodge, 543-2855, write to the Grand Teton Lodge Company, Box 240, Moran, WY 83013; Flagg Ranch, 543-2861 or 733-8761, Box 187, Moran, WY 83013; Moose Enterprises, Inc. (prefer monthly rental), (307) 733-3863, Box 331, Moose, WY 83012; Signal Mountain Lodge, 543-2831 or 733-5470, Box 50, Moran, WY 83013; and Triangle X Ranch (weekly, American plan) 733-2183, Box 120T, Moose, WY 83012. Most of these also provide meals to non-guests. Groceries are sold at Colter Bay, Flagg Ranch, Kelly, Jenny Lake, Moose, and Signal Mountain. For information on commercial enterprises outside the park, write to the chamber of commerce address or the Wyoming Travel Commission address.

Post offices. Post offices are located at Colter Bay (summer only), Moran, Moose, and Kelly.

Hiking

You may think time is fixed but it's not. Its many speeds here include car time, float time, horseback time, and hiking time. Car time is, well, just car time. Hiking time is Grand Teton time, Jackson Hole time, your time. On great days it's timeless time. There are more than 225 miles of hiking trails in the park.

The shortest trails are the self-guiding trails 0.5 to 2 miles long. See the list under Ranger-led Activities. The valley trails that run along the base of the Teton Range and take you to the large lakes in front of the mountains are also shorter and less arduous than the mountain trails. The valley trails will pique your interest and help you decide if you wish to hike further into the mountains. You can take a half-day to all-day hike into the canyons between Teton peaks. The walking will be more difficult, requiring some up- and downhill effort, but the rewards— mountain views, wildflowers, and wildlife—are worth it. You can take multiple-day trips over highcountry passes and into the alpine zone. A free backcountry permit is required for all overnight camping.

In the visitor centers you can buy the *Teton Trails* guide booklet. It offers shaded relief trail maps, lengths and hiking estimates, scenery identification drawings, and photographs on which you can trace your route. Rangers can direct you to interesting hikes and help you assess the level of difficulty. If you plan to travel off trail you must register at Jenny Lake Ranger Station, or at the Moose Visitor Center from October through May. Overnight travel requires a free backcountry use permit (see Backcountry Basics).

Wear comfortable and sturdy footgear no matter how far you hope to travel. Even on shorter hikes, be sure to carry raingear. Afternoon thundershowers are common throughout the hiking season and can occur suddenly. The day may be sunny and warm, but a quick drenching rain can spell big trouble for hikers without raingear. Life-threatening hypothermia occurs most often in the 30 to 40°F temperature range, especially if clothing is wet and there is some wind. Be prepared. Don't take chances. You will also need to carry water on your hike. At high altitudes the sun is hot and the humidity is low; you get thirsty quickly. Microorganisms in stream water can cause intestinal problems 10-14 days after you drink, so use your canteen. (See Water Warning under Backcountry Basics.) Be sure to carry lunch and some high-energy snacks to munch on while you walk. Add sunglasses, sunscreen, a hat, and camera, and you will be prepared to enjoy your day on the trail.

Please read Bear Warning under Backcountry Basics. Pets are not permitted on trails or in the backcountry. Most valley trails are open by early June. Highcountry trails may remain closed by snow until mid-July. Please note that horse parties have the right-of-way on trails. Step well off the trail and remain quiet while horses pass.

Some of the park's most intriguing aspects reveal themselves only to hikers.

Backcountry Basics

Most basic is this: *Overnight backcountry use requires a free backcountry use permit.* This written permit can be obtained at Moose Visitor Center, open all year, or at Jenny Lake Ranger Station and Colter Bay Visitor Center in summer, on a first-come, first-served basis. There are more people who want a wilderness experience than there is wilderness in the park, so backcountry user capacities have been established. This means that some people are turned away. Reservations may be made for backcountry camping areas by mail only from January 1 to June 1. These reservations by mail are available for only 30 percent of the backcountry camping sites. From June 1 to October 1, no reservations can be made, and then all unreserved sites are first-come, first-served. Organized groups wishing to backpack overnight should write the Permits Office at the park address for full particulars.

Making a Reservation. Submit your *final* itinerary listing the specific sites at which you wish to stay each night (list calendar dates!) and the size of your group (the maximum group size is 12) to the Permits Office at the Park address. See Closed Areas below. You must still pick up your permit in person by 10 a.m. of the day your trip begins. A backcountry zone system is used to minimize human impact and to allow you freer choice in camping. The Teton Range above 7,000 feet elevation has been divided into camping zones. You may stay anywhere within a zone if you follow these simple rules: 1. No ground fires are allowed. Small backpacking stoves are recommended for cooking. 2. Camp at least one mile away from any trail junction or patrol cabin. 3. Camp at least 100 feet away from all lakes and

Backpackers can readily reach the heart of the Tetons and enjoy pristine wilderness. Good backcountry ethics ensure protection of these wild places and minimize conflicts with bears.

streams. 4. Camp out of sight of the trail and other campers. 5. Do not camp in fragile or overused sites that will show signs of your camp having been there (unless told otherwise).

Below the 7,000-foot level there are a few remaining designated lakeside backcountry camping sites. Unless there is a fire danger, wood fires are permitted in the firegrates provided at these designated camping sites.

General Backcountry Regulations. Pets, firearms, and wheeled vehicles are not permitted. Carry out all refuse and leave no evidence of your stay. Short-cutting on trails is prohibited. Keep stock out of camping areas. Use hitch racks where provided. Do not tie stock to live trees. To prevent pollution, do not wash dishes or laundry in, and do not bathe in, lakes and streams.

Closed Areas. When you pick up your permit, check on areas that may be closed to backcountry use. No overnight camping is permitted at Lake Solitude, Bradley Lake, Taggart Lake, Laurel Lake, Amphitheater Lake, below the Forks of Cascade Canyon to Jenny Lake, and the lower valley area east of the Valley Trail and the east shore of Jackson Lake. No overnight camping is permitted along the Snake River.

Water Warning. Surface water is of questionable purity. Carry water from approved public supplies. Backcountry water should be boiled for one minute, three to five minutes at higher altitudes. Water treatment disinfection chemicals are not considered as reliable as boiling to safeguard against *Giardia* and *Campylobacter* intestinal disorders. Most water filter mechanisms are not adequate for these organisms. The eve-

ning meal is an ideal time to boil water for drinking and brushing teeth and for the next day's use.

Bear Warning. Black bears are sometimes seen in the backcountry and in campgrounds. They show little fear of people and may try to get your food. Federal law requires proper food storage in the backcountry and in campgrounds. Suspend food from a tree (or bear pole if provided) or store it out of sight in a vehicle. Your backcountry permit packet includes instructions on hanging your food. A bear brochure is available free at ranger stations and visitor centers. Make sure everyone in your party reads this information before your trip. Report all bear sightings, damage, or injury to a park ranger. Grizzly bears are seen occasionally in northern parts of the park. If a bear should charge you, climb a tree or play dead. Don't try to run away, however. Running excites the bear, and you cannot outrun one.

Theft from Parked Cars. Trailhead parking areas are patrolled regularly, but in recent years theft from cars parked overnight has become more common. Leave nothing of value visible in your car and thoroughly lock up the vehicle before leaving on your hike. It's best to lock valuables in your trunk.

Trip Planning. Write the Grand Teton Natural History Association at the park address for a list of sales literature and maps to enhance your pre-trip planning and enjoyment.

Horseback Riding. For short rides with a guide you can rent saddle horses at Jenny Lake, Colter Bay, Flagg Ranch, and Jackson Lake Lodge. Jenny Lake Lodge and the Triangle X Ranch have

Overnight backcountry travel with horses requires a backcountry permit. Please observe the regulations on horse use. They are designed to protect fragile landscapes.

horses for guests only. A short horseback ride gives you a leisurely look at the park and a sample of Jackson Hole's Old West flavor. If you've never ridden, or have not ridden in years, *make the first ride short.* Your first steps after first riding a horse for an hour or more feel very strange! The concessioners offer a variety of wagon rides and hayrides to cowboy cookouts. Guided trips of several days can be arranged with park concessioners. Or you can write the chamber of commerce address for information about area outfitters. If you plan to bring your own stock, write the chief ranger at the park address for information on saddle and pack animal use regulations. Also read the Backcountry Basics section. Please note that no grazing is permitted in the park; processed feed must be packed in. Saddle and pack animal facilities are available only at String Lake Parking Area, Whitegrass Ranger Station, and the Granite Canyon, Sheffield Creek, Arizona Creek, and Pilgrim Creek trailheads. Many highcountry trails are blocked by snow until mid-July and are impassable to saddle and pack animals. For this reason many horse parties camp on the adjoining national forests and take day-trips into Grand Teton National Park.

Mountaineering

This is one of the country's finest areas for general mountaineering. The rock is mostly excellent, snow slopes mostly moderate, and the range unusually accessible. Still, many climbers pack in and set up their camps in a high-country location. Mountaineering guide service and instruction are available at Jenny Lake. Write to: Exum Guide Service and School of American Mountaineering, Box 56, Moose, WY 83012. Jackson Hole Mountain Guides also offers guide services in the park; write to Box 7477, Jackson, WY 83001. Climbing guidebooks and individual route guides are available by mail from the Grand Teton Natural History Association address or can be purchased at park visitor centers and the Jenny Lake Ranger Station.

The Jenny Lake Ranger Station (see map) is the center for climbing information and registration in the park from early June to mid-September. Climbing conditions are the best from mid-July through late September, although afternoon thundershowers are common in these months and an extended period of poor weather with snowfall usually occurs in late August. May and June feature long periods of poor weather with heavy precipitation, some snow, and subfreezing temperatures. Heavy rockfall and some avalanche activity are common. Major storms occur in late September and early October with snowfall and icing conditions on most routes. Winter weather in the Teton Range is severe: heavy snowfall, high winds, and extreme temperatures. Avalanche danger, usually present, is frequently high December to June.

Registration and Information. Because of the hazards and possibility of acci-

Hard, crystalline rock and an alpine panorama make the Teton Range a mountaineering mecca.

dents in mountaineering, the National Park Service requires all climbers to register in person before climbing and to sign out in person after climbing. From early June to mid-September this is done at the Jenny Lake Ranger Station. It must be done at Moose Visitor Center the rest of the year. Notes left at the ranger station are not acceptable registration or sign-outs. (Climbers returning after the ranger station is closed may sign out at the Late-Returning Climbers Registration Box on the ranger station porch.) Registration is regulated under the Federal Code of Regulations. The mountaineering rangers on duty provide current information on the nature and condition of climbing routes, equipment and experience requirements, and time factors. Request general mountaineering information from the chief ranger at the park address.

Guidebooks, maps, and photographs of various peaks and routes are available at the Jenny Lake Ranger Station to help you plan climbs. In winter — mid-September through May — information and registration are available at the Moose Visitor Center. Conventional mountaineering equipment is satisfactory for summer climbs. Ice axes are essential and crampons may be desirable for early season climbs and for some routes throughout the season. Climbing helmets are strongly recommended for technical climbs and for climbs exposed to regular rockfall dangers. Climbing equipment and food suitable for backpacking may be purchased in the area. Limited selections of rental equipment may be available. Low cost lodging for registered climbers is available at Grand Teton Climber's Ranch, an American Alpine Club-operated concession. Write the manager at Moose, WY 83012.

Boating and Floating

Boat trips are offered by concessioners on Jackson and Jenny lakes. These vary from steak fry cruises to lunch excursions, to drop-off and pick-up cruises for hiking trips up Cascade Canyon. On Jackson Lake concessioners operate Colter Bay Marina, Leek's Marina, and Signal Mountain Marina. Marinas offer fishing guide service, launching, marine supplies and fuel, buoy rentals, and canoe rentals. Teton Boating Company provides cruises, shuttle service, and boat rental on Jenny Lake. Canoe rentals for lake use only are available from Moose Enterprises at the grocery store in Moose.

Floating. One of the best ways to experience the park's wildlife and scenery is by floating the Snake River. Numerous concessioners offer guided float trips in inflatable rubber rafts. Outfitters are listed in *Teewinot,* or write to the park address for a complete list. (Please don't ask National Park Service employees to recommend one over another.) On a float trip you don't have to watch the trail or mind the horse. You just watch the animals and scenery and listen to the guide's narrative, wildlife identifications, and local lore. The Teton Range appears to slide by, now peeking above a massive river-cut glacial moraine, now peeking through trees, now disappearing from view. Morning and evening floats are best for seeing wildlife. You may well see bald eagles, ospreys, moose, great blue herons, Canada Geese, beaver, otters, and various ducks. You can float the river in your own craft, but a permit is required. The river is floated in the park from 1,000 feet below Jackson Lake Dam to Moose, a distance of about 25 miles. Do not attempt the river on your own below Pacific Creek (see map) unless you are familiar with

your craft—kayaks, inflatables, and canoes are best—and experienced on rivers of similar difficulty and similar hazards. People too often underestimate the power of the Snake. Write the park address for information about hazards, regulations, equipment, and travel times in floating the Snake River in the park. Motorized craft are not permitted on the Snake River.

The park's numerous lakes and the Snake River offer many boating and floating opportunities.

Fishing

Fishing is regulated in keeping with the park's overall management objective of maintaining natural systems and scenic values. Most park waters are open in season, subject to Wyoming laws and National Park Service regulations. These regulations are intended to maintain quality waters, protect natural fish populations, and protect the food sources of bald eagles, ospreys, otters, great blue herons, and other native fish-eating wildlife. A Wyoming fishing license is required and may be purchased in the park at the Colter Bay or Moose Tackle Shops, at Signal Mountain, and at Leek's Marina. Information on fishing laws and on special regulations, including bait restrictions, closed waters, artificial fly fishing waters, and creel limits is available at the visitor centers. You must check on this information before you fish. Fishing guides are available at the lodges.

The park's waters support one of the last wild inland populations of cutthroat trout. The Snake River cutthroat, a unique race of the cutthroat species, is the only trout native to the park. (See pages 56-57.) The National Park Service encourages you to release small cutthroat carefully so that the opportunity to catch this unusual fish is perpetuated. Other gamefish include rainbow, lake (Mackinaw), brown, and brook trout and the Rocky Mountain whitefish.

The use or possession of fish eggs — real or artificial — or fish as bait in any park waters are prohibited. (Some dead non-game fish are permitted on the shores of Jackson Lake only.) Get specifics at a visitor center or write the chief ranger at the park address for fishing regulations and information.

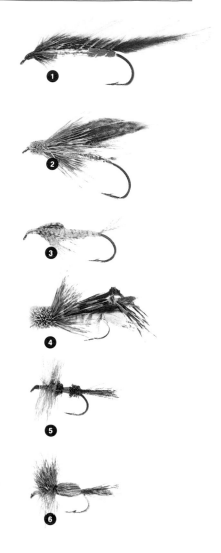

The Snake River offers world famous angling for cutthroat trout. Catch-and-release angling is encouraged. Popular artificial fly patterns here are: 1 Silver Spruce Matuka, 2 Muddler Minnow, 3 Matts Fur Nymph, 4 Jay-Davis Hopper, 5 Royal Wulff, and 6 Yellow Humpy.

Winter Activities

Winter activities gear up in mid-December. Just one good storm can turn Jackson Hole into a winter wonderland covered with up to 6 feet of snow in some years. In or near the park you can then crosscountry ski, ice fish, snowshoe, mountaineer, ice skate, snowmobile, and observe wildlife and scenery. Minor park roads are not plowed in winter. The Teton Park Road (see map) is closed from Cottonwood Creek bridge to Signal Mountain Lodge. There is no direct car access between Moose and Teton Village. Yellowstone National Park roads are not plowed in winter.

Registration and information on oversnow travel are available at the Moose Visitor Center. Off-season camping is available at Colter Bay across from the visitor center, which provides restrooms and water. Lodging is available in winter at Flagg Ranch in Rockefeller Parkway and at Triangle X Ranch in the park. Nearby Jackson offers full tourist services year round. Write the chamber of commerce address for information.

But you must prepare for the weather. An average 4-foot base of snow in the valley is much deeper in the mountains. Daytime temperatures range from $-25°$ to $+50°$F. Severe winter storms and blizzards can occur throughout the season. All oversnow travel is prohibited in the Snake River bottom between Moose and Moran as well as in the Willow Flats at Jackson Lake Lodge. Check at the Moose Visitor Center for exact boundaries on these closed areas.

Winter sports wait only for that first good snow. Moose Visitor Center is the registration point for winter activities, including mountaineering.

Management Concerns and Safety

Many management concerns and safety tips are given under specific subjects in this handbook. Here are other things to consider. Camp only in designated sites. Obtain a backcountry use permit for all overnight backcountry use, including in winter. Register at the Jenny Lake Ranger Station in summer or park headquarters in winter before starting any off-trail hike or climb. Boat permits are required for the use of any watercraft on park waters. Fishing requires a Wyoming license, and please check park regulations at a visitor center. Obtain an oversnow vehicle permit at Moose Visitor Center and check the regulations before operating a snowmobile or snowplane in the park. Bicycles are not allowed on trails or in the backcountry. **Pets must be leashed and under physical restraint at all times. They are not permitted on trails, in buildings, or in the backcountry.** Kennels are found in Jackson; check with the chamber of commerce. All natural features are protected; leave all rocks and plants in their natural setting. All park animals, including bears, are wild and protected by law. Do not feed or molest them. Please read the Bear Warning under Backcountry Basics.

Driving Tips. Drive carefully and defensively, especially at dawn, dusk, and at night. Every season large animals are killed and vehicles are mangled. Slow down, and ask passengers to help spot animals in the road. When stopping to view wildlife, stop in turnouts, be careful to stop your vehicle in the safest position possible, with all doors shut. Consider traffic flow problems and their potential hazard. Be a responsible driver. Keep motor vehicles off bikeways. Report all accidents to a park ranger. Observe posted speed limits.

Respect Wildlife. Keep a respectful distance from all animals to avoid disturbing their natural routine, especially when taking pictures. Larger animals are quick, powerful, and unpredictable. Getting too close can result in serious injury. Take special care to avoid encounters with bears and to help maintain their natural fear of humans. Many small mammals can carry diseases and should never be touched or handled. All animals are part of the natural processes protected within the park. Allow them to find their own food. Their natural diet insures their health and survival. *Feeding wild animals is prohibited no matter how convincingly they beg.*

Fire Management. The park is zoned for the management of natural fire. In some parts of the park lightning-caused fires are monitored and allowed to burn, because we have learned that natural fire often plays a vital role in an ecosystem. Some plant species require fire to thrive, and several animal species benefit from fire. Natural fires that threaten developed areas will be extinguished to protect human life and property. Report fires to a park ranger. Human-caused fires will be extinguished. Please be careful with fire yourself.

Nearby Attractions

The park abuts other expanses of wild country. A photographer fills her frame with elk at Yellowstone; a backpacker enjoys the Targhee National Forest; and National Elk Refuge visitors watch the herd from sleighs.

John D. Rockefeller, Jr., Memorial Parkway joins Grand Teton National Park with **Yellowstone National Park.** Yellowstone is world famous as the first national park. Its geysers and mudpots, canyons and waterfalls, and wildlife and wilderness are spectacular. For information write or call the Superintendent, Yellowstone National Park, P.O. Box 168, Yellowstone National Park, WY 82190, (307) 344-7381.

Teton National Forest, Teton Wilderness, and Targhee National Forest adjoin the park boundary. For information about hunting, fishing, backpacking, and campgrounds write or call the Forest Supervisor, Bridger-Teton National Forest, Box 1888, Jackson, WY 83001, (307) 733-2752, or Forest Supervisor, Targhee National Forest, Box 208, St. Anthony, ID 83445, (208) 624-3151.

National Elk Refuge headquarters is just east of Jackson (see map). Christmas through April 1 you can ride a horsedrawn sleigh into North America's largest elk herd. In summer you can drive on the refuge road into the sagebrush and buttes landscape. For information write or call the Refuge Manager, National Elk Refuge, Box C, Jackson WY 83001, (307) 733-9212.

Jackson National Fish Hatchery Visitor Center lies across the highway from the southernmost park boundary (see map). This hatchery raises trout. Anglers can go stark raving mad over the seething masses of trout in the hatchery ponds. For information write or call the Hatchery Manager, Jackson National Fish Hatchery, Box 1845, Jackson WY 83001, (307) 733-2510.

Armchair Explorations

The nonprofit Grand Teton Natural History Association, Moose, WY 83012 sells books, maps, and other publications in support of the interpretive and management programs of the national park. These items are displayed at the visitor centers, or can be purchased by mail. Write for a free list. The following selected book list may also be of interest.

Betts, Robert B. *Along the Ramparts of the Tetons: The Saga of Jackson Hole,* Colorado Associated University Press, 1978.

Clark, Tim W. *Ecology of Jackson Hole,* Jackson, Wyo., 1981.

Crandall, Hugh. *Grand Teton: The Story Behind the Scenery,* KC Publications.

Fryxell, Fritiof. *Mountaineering in the Tetons,* The Teton Bookshop, 1978.

Harry, Bryan. *Teton Trails,* Grand Teton Natural History Association, 1961.

Harry, Bryan. *Wildlife of Yellowstone and Grand Teton National Parks,* Wheelwright Press Ltd., 1972.

Hayden, Elizabeth Wied. *From Trapper to Tourist in Jackson Hole,* Grand Teton Natural History Association, 1981.

Love, J.D. et al. *Geologic Block Diagram,* Grand Teton Natural History Association/ U.S. Geological Survey, 1973.

Love, J.D. and John C. Reed, Jr. *Creation of the Teton Landscape,* Grand Teton Natural History Association, 1968.

Murie, Olaus J. *Elk of North America,* Teton Bookshop, 1979.

Righter, Robert W. *Crucible for Conservation: The Creation of Grand Teton National Park,* Colorado Associated University Press, 1982.

Saylor David, J. *Jackson Hole Wyoming: In the Shadow of the Tetons,* University of Oklahoma Press, 1971.

Schreier, Carl. *Explorer's Guide to Grand Teton National Park,* Homestead Publishing, 1982.

Schullery, Paul. *The Bears of Yellowstone,* Yellowstone Library and Museum Association, 1980.

Shaw, Richard J. *Plants of Yellowstone and Grand Teton National Parks,* Utah State University Press, 1976.

Yandell, Michael D. *National Parkways: Grand Teton National Parkways,* Worldwide Research and Publishing Co.

Index

Numbers in italics refer to photographs, illustrations, or maps.

Handbook 122

The National Park Service expresses its appreciation
to all those persons who made the preparation and
production of this handbook possible. The Service
also thanks the Grand Teton Natural History Association for its financial support of this project.
All photos and artwork not credited below come
from the files of Grand Teton National Park.

Greg Beaumont 13,30 photo, 36 photos, 58, 60-61,
66-67 yellowthroat, towhee, goose, crane, jay, owl,
killdeer, snipe, 68-69 columbine, dandelion, sugarbowl,
lily, gentian, flax, geranium, phlox, paintbrush,
64-65 weasel, pika, marmots, mouse
Erwin and Peggy Bauer 70-71, 82 top and middle,
87 middle, 88, 93 top
P. Billing 15
Bridger-Teton National Forest 93 middle
Franz J. Camenzind 56 inset
John Clymer 52-53
John Dawson 36-37 paintings
Denver Public Library 54 inset
Jim Elder 78 campers, 87 bottom
Jeff Foott 66-77 goshawk, grouse, eagle, 68-69 orchid,
violet, 64-65 elk
Jackie Gilmore 44 inset, 64-65 moose, beaver, squirrel
High Country Flies 89
Jerry D. Jacka 77 top and bottom
Frances Judge 47 inset
Stephen J. Krasemann 64-65 bear, hare, bobcat
Russell Lamb covers, 4-5, 16-17, 24, 40-41
Wayne Lankinen 64-65 deer
David Muench 6, 18-19, 22-23, 32-33, 48
National Elk Refuge 93 bottom
National Geographic (David Alan Harvey) 10-11, 44-45
Boyd Norton 34
Leigh Ortenburger 35 diagram
Jaime Quintero 28-29
Smithsonian Institution (William H. Jackson) 55 inset
Teton County Library 46-47
Triangle X Ranch, 42 top